Table of Contents

Introduction 3
Protein 3
Nutritional Value Of Protein 4
    Protein Foods 5
    How To Get Your Protein Needs 6
    Getting More Protein Into Your Day, Naturally 8
    Protein – Maintaining Muscle Mass As You Age 10
        Protein Shakes, Powders And Supplements 11
        Protein And Exercise 11
        Very High Protein Diets Are Dangerous 12
        The Health Benefits Of Protein 13
High-quality Vs. Low-quality Protein 14
    How Much High-Quality Protein Do You Need? 15
    Good Sources Of High-quality Protein 15
        Tips To Increase Your Protein Intake 17
        Protein Powders, Shakes, And Bars 18
    Using Protein Supplements 19
High Protein Foods 20
    Other Types Of Cheese That Are High In Protein 23
    Whey Protein Supplements 26

Other High Protein Legumes 27

High Protein Recipes 31

Miniature Omelettes With Ricotta 31

Herbed Chicken Skewers 32

Dippy Eggs With Marmite Soldiers 34

Spiced Scrambled Eggs 34

Thai Salmon Kebabs With Sweet Chilli & Lime Dip 35

One-Pan English Breakfast 36

Salmon & soya bean salad 37

Vitality Chicken Salad With Avocado Dressing 38

Griddled Chicken With quinoa Greek Salad 39

Cajun Turkey Steaks With Pineapple Salsa 41

Spicy Cajun Chicken quinoa 42

Spring Salmon With Minty Veg 43

Simple Seafood Chowder 44

Sea Bass & Seafood Italian One-Pot 46

Fruity LAMB TAGINE 47

Chicken, Red Pepper & Almond Traybake 48

Mexican Bean Chilli 50

Conclusion 51

Introduction

Protein is a nutrient your body needs to grow and repair cells and to work properly.Protein is found in a wide range of food and it's important that you get enough protein in your diet every day. How much protein you need from your diet varies depending on your weight, gender, age and health.

Protein

Protein provides energy and supports your mood and cognitive function. It's a vital nutrient required for building, maintaining, and repairing tissues, cells, and organs throughout the body.While it's in many of the foods that we eat every day, for something so common it's often a misunderstood part of our diets.

When you eat protein, it is broken down into the 20 amino acids that are the body's basic building blocks for growth and energy. The amino acid tryptophan influences mood by producing serotonin, which can reduce symptoms of depression and anxiety and improve overall cognitive function.

Most animal sources of protein, such as meat, poultry, fish, eggs, and dairy, deliver all the amino acids your body needs, while plant-based protein sources such as grains, beans, vegetables, and nuts often lack one or more of the essential amino acids. However, that doesn't mean you have to eat animal products to get the right amino acids. By eating a variety of plant-based sources of protein each day you can ensure your body gets all the essential amino acids it needs.

Nutritional Value Of Protein

The nutritional value of a protein is measured by the quantity of essential amino acids it contains.

Different foods contain different amounts of essential amino acids. Generally:

- Animal products (such as chicken, beef or fish and dairy products) have all of the essential amino acids and are known as 'complete' protein (or ideal or high-quality protein).
- Soy products, quinoa and the seed of a leafy green called amaranth (consumed in Asia and the Mediterranean) also have all of the essential amino acids.

- Plant proteins (beans, lentils, nuts and whole grains) usually lack at least one of the essential amino acids and are considered 'incomplete' proteins.
- People following a strict vegetarian or vegan diet need to choose a variety of protein sources from a combination of plant foods every day to make sure they get an adequate mix of essential amino acids.
- If you follow a vegetarian or vegan diet, as long as you eat a wide variety of foods, you can usually get the protein you need. For example, a meal containing cereals and legumes, such as baked beans on toast, provides all the essential amino acids found in a typical meat dish.

Protein Foods

Some food sources of dietary protein include:

- Lean meats – beef, lamb, veal, pork, kangaroo
- Poultry – chicken, turkey, duck, emu, goose, bush birds
- Fish and seafood – fish, prawns, crab, lobster, mussels, oysters, scallops, clams
- Eggs

- Dairy products – milk, yoghurt (especially greek yoghurt), cheese (especially cottage cheese)
- Nuts (including nut pastes) and seeds – almonds, pine nuts, walnuts, macadamias, hazelnuts, cashews, pumpkin seeds, sesame seeds, sunflower seeds
- Legumes and beans – all beans, lentils, chickpeas, split peas, tofu.

Some grain and cereal-based products are also sources of protein, but are generally not as high in protein as meat and meat-alternative products.

How To Get Your Protein Needs

Your daily protein needs can easily be met by following the Australian Dietary Guidelines. The Guidelines group foods into five different food groups, each of which provide key nutrients.

The two main food groups that contribute to protein are the:

- 'Lean meat and poultry, fish, eggs, tofu, nuts and seeds and legumes/beans' group
- 'milk, yoghurt, cheese and/or alternatives (mostly reduced fat)' group.

As part of a healthy diet, the Guidelines recommend particular serves per day from each of the five food groups.

The human body can't store protein and will excrete any excess, so the most effective way of meeting your daily protein requirement is to eat small amounts at every meal.

So, what is a serve? A standard serving size of 'lean meat and poultry, fish, eggs, nuts and seeds, and legumes/beans' is one of:

- 65g cooked lean meats such as beef, lamb, veal, pork, goat or kangaroo (about 90 to 100g raw)
- 80g cooked lean poultry such as chicken or turkey (100g raw)
- 100g cooked fish fillet (about 115g raw weight) or one small can of fish
- 2 large eggs
- 1 cup (150g) cooked dried beans, lentils, chickpeas, split peas or canned beans (preferably with no added salt)
- 170g tofu
- 30g nuts, seeds, peanut or almond butter or tahini or other nut or seed paste (no added salt).

A serve of 'milk, yoghurt, cheese and/or alternatives (mostly reduced fat)' could include:

- 250ml (1 cup) fresh, UHT long life, reconstituted powdered milk or buttermilk
- 120ml (1/2 cup) evaporated milk
- 200g (3/4 cup or 1 small carton) yoghurt
- 40g (2 slices) hard cheese such as cheddar
- 120g (1/2 cup) ricotta cheese.

Getting More Protein Into Your Day, Naturally

If you're looking for ways to get more protein into your diet, here are some suggestions:

- Try a peanut butter sandwich. Remember to use natural peanut butter (or any other nut paste) with no added salt, sugar or other fillers.
- Low-fat cottage or ricotta cheese is high in protein and can go in your scrambled eggs, casserole, mashed potato or pasta dish. Or spread it on your toast in the morning.
- Nuts and seeds are fantastic in salads, with vegetables and served on top of curries. Try toasting some pine

nuts or flaked almonds and putting them in your green salad.
- Beans are great in soups, casseroles, and pasta sauces. Try tipping a drained can of cannellini beans into your favourite vegetable soup recipe or casserole.
- A plate of hummus and freshly cut vegetable sticks as a snack or hummus spread on your sandwich will give you easy extra protein at lunchtime.
- Greek yoghurt is a protein rich food that you can use throughout the day. Add some on your favourite breakfast cereal, put a spoonful on top of a bowl of pumpkin soup or serve it as dessert with some fresh fruit.
- Eggs are a versatile and easy option that can be enjoyed on their own or mixed in a variety of dishes.
- Getting too little protein (protein deficiency)
- Protein deficiency means not getting enough protein in your diet. Protein deficiency is rare in Australia, as the Australian diet generally includes far more protein than we actually need.
- However, protein deficiency may occur in people with special requirements, such as older people and people following strict vegetarian or vegan diets.

Symptoms of protein deficiency include:

- Wasting and shrinkage of muscle tissue
- Oedema (build-up of fluids, particularly in the feet and ankles)
- Anaemia (the blood's inability to deliver sufficient oxygen to the cells, usually caused by dietary deficiencies such as lack of iron)
- Slow growth (in children).

Protein – Maintaining Muscle Mass As You Age

From around 50 years of age, humans begin to gradually lose skeletal muscle. This is known as sarcopenia and is common in older people. Loss of muscle mass is worsened by chronic illness, poor diet and inactivity.

Meeting the daily recommended protein intake may help you maintain muscle mass and strength. This is important for maintaining your ability to walk and reducing your risk of injury from falls.

To maintain muscle mass, it's important for older people to eat protein 'effectively'. This means consuming high-quality protein foods, such as lean meats.

Protein Shakes, Powders And Supplements

Protein shakes, powders and supplements are unnecessary for most Australians' health needs. According to the most recent national nutrition survey, 99% of Australians get enough protein through the food they eat.

Any protein you eat on top of what your body needs will either be excreted from your body as waste, or stored as weight gain.

The best way for you to get the protein you need is to eat a wide variety of protein-rich foods as outlined in the Australian Dietary Guidelines, as part of a balanced diet. But if you are still interested in using protein shakes, powders and supplements, talk to your doctor.

Protein And Exercise

Soon after exercising, it's recommended that you have a serve of high-quality protein (such as a glass of milk or tub of yoghurt) with a carbohydrate meal to help maintain your body's protein balance. Studies have shown this to be good for you, even after low to moderate aerobic exercise (such as walking), particularly for older adults.

People who exercise vigorously or are trying to put on muscle mass do not need to consume extra protein. High-protein diets do not lead to increased muscle mass. It's the stimulation of muscle tissue through exercise, not extra dietary protein, which leads to muscle growth.

Studies show that weight-trainers who do not eat extra protein (either in food or protein powders) still gain muscle at the same rate as weight-trainers who supplement their diets with protein.

Very High Protein Diets Are Dangerous

Some fad diets promote very high protein intakes of between 200 and 400g per day. This is more than five times the amount recommended in the Australian Dietary Guidelines.

The protein recommendations in the Guidelines provide enough protein to build and repair muscles, even for body builders and athletes.

A very high-protein diet can strain the kidneys and liver. It can also prompt excessive loss of the mineral calcium, which can increase your risk of osteoporosis.

The Health Benefits Of Protein

Protein gives you the energy to get up and go—and keep going. While too much protein can be harmful to people with kidney disease, diabetes, and some other conditions, eating the right amount of high-quality protein:

- Keeps your immune system functioning properly, maintains heart health and your respiratory system, and speeds recovery after exercise
- Is vital to the growth and development of children and for maintaining health in your senior years
- Can help reduce your risk for diabetes and cardiovascular disease
- Can help you think clearly and may improve recall
- Can improve your mood and boost your resistance to stress, anxiety, and depression
- May help you maintain a healthy weight by curbing appetite, making you feel full longer, and fueling you with extra energy for exercising.

As well as being imperative to feeling healthy and energetic, protein is also important to the way you look. Eating high-quality protein can help you maintain healthy skin, nails, and hair, build muscle, and maintain lean body mass while dieting.

While most people eating a Western diet get sufficient quantity of protein each day, many of us are not getting the quality of protein we need.

High-quality Vs. Low-quality Protein

Distinguishing between industrially raised meat and organic, grass-fed meat is only part of separating low- and high-quality sources of protein.

While some processed or lunch meats, for example, can be a good source of protein, many are loaded with salt, which can cause high blood pressure and lead to other health problems.

Processed meats have also been linked with an increased risk of cancer, likely due to the substances used in the processing of the meat.

The key to ensuring you eat sufficient high-quality protein is to include different types in your diet, rather than relying on just red or processed meat.

How Much High-Quality Protein Do You Need?

Adults should eat at least 0.8g of protein per kilogram (2.2lb) of body weight per day. That means a 180lb man should eat at least 65 grams of high-quality protein per day. A higher intake may help to lower your risk for obesity, osteoporosis, type 2 diabetes, and stroke.

Nursing women need about 20 grams more of high-quality protein a day than they did before pregnancy to support milk production.

Older adults should aim for 1 to 1.5 grams of protein for each kilogram of weight (think 0.5g of protein per lb. of body weight if that's easier).

Try to divide your protein intake equally among meals.

Good Sources Of High-quality Protein

Fish. Most seafood is high in protein and low in saturated fat. Fish such as salmon, trout, sardines, anchovies, sablefish (black cod), and herring are also high in omega-3 fatty acids. Experts recommend eating seafood at least twice a week.

Poultry. Removing the skin from chicken and turkey can substantially reduce the saturated fat. In the U.S., non-organic poultry may also contain antibiotics and been raised on GMO feed grown with pesticides, so opt for organic and free-range if possible.

Dairy Products. Products such as skim milk, cheese, and yoghurt offer lots of healthy protein. Beware of added sugar in low-fat yoghurts and flavored milk, though, and skip processed cheese that often contains non-dairy ingredients.

Beans. Beans and peas are packed full of both protein and fiber. Add them to salads, soups and stews to boost your protein intake.

Nuts And Seeds. As well as being rich sources of protein, nuts and seeds are also high in fiber and "good" fats. Add to salads or keep handy for snacks.

Tofu And Soy Products. Non-GMO tofu and soy are excellent red meat alternatives, high in protein and low in fat. Try a "meatless Monday," plant-based protein sources are often less expensive than meat so it can be as good for your wallet as it is for your health.

Tips To Increase Your Protein Intake

To include more high-quality protein in your diet, try replacing processed carbs with high-quality protein. It can reduce your risk for heart disease and stroke, and you'll also feel full longer, which can help you maintain a healthy weight.

Reduce the amount of processed carbohydrates you consume—from foods such as pastries, cakes, pizza, cookies and chips—and replace them with fish, beans, nuts, seeds, peas, chicken, dairy, and soy and tofu products.

Snack on nuts and seeds instead of chips, replace a baked dessert with Greek yogurt, or swap out slices of pizza for a grilled chicken breast and a side of beans.

Not A Seafood Fan? Make Fish More Palatable

If you're not a fan of seafood, but want to include more in your diet, there are ways to make fish more palatable.

- Always buy fresh fish. Some say tilapia, cod, or salmon have the least "fishy" taste.
- Disguise the taste by adding a flavorful sauce.
- Marinate fish with Creole or Cajun seasoning.
- Add shell fish or white fish, such as cod or tilapia, to a curry.

- Combine grilled fish with fresh salsa or your favorite chutney
- Mix canned salmon or tuna with low-fat mayonnaise and chopped onion for a tasty sandwich filling.
- To avoid problems when increasing protein intake
- Choose unsalted nuts and seeds, to reduce your daily sodium intake.
- When shopping for canned beans, choose the low sodium versions.
- Adding more protein to your diet can increase urine output, so drink plenty of water to stay hydrated.
- Increasing protein can also cause calcium loss so make sure to get plenty of calcium (1,000 to 1,200 mg per day).

Protein Powders, Shakes, And Bars

In most cases, consuming the right balance of whole foods each day will provide you with all the nutrients you need, negating the need for protein supplements. However, you may benefit from supplementing your diet if you're:

- An adult switching to a vegan diet—eliminating meat, chicken, fish, and even dairy and eggs from your diet

- An older adult with a small appetite who finds it difficult to eat your protein requirements in whole foods
- Starting or increasing a regular workout program, trying to add muscle, recovering from a sports injury, or find you feel weak while exercising or lifting weights

Using Protein Supplements

Protein supplements come in various forms including powders you mix with milk or water, pre-mixed, ready-to-drink shakes, or in bars. The most common types of protein used are whey, casein, and soy. Whey and casein are milk-based proteins, while soy is the better choice for vegans or anyone with a dairy allergy.

Safety Concerns. Protein supplements may not be safe for older people with renal disease or people who have recently undergone surgery on the digestive system. Some ingredients may even interact with prescription medication, so check with your doctor or pharmacist before using.

Drink plenty of water to stay hydrated and make sure you're getting enough calcium in your diet.

Look Out For Extra Ingredients. Many protein bars are packed with carbs and added sugar.

High Protein Foods

If you buy something through a link on this page, we may earn a small commission. How this works.

Protein makes up the building blocks of organs, muscles, skin, and hormones. Your body needs protein to maintain and repair tissues. Meanwhile, children need it for growth. Studies show that eating protein can also help you lose weight and belly fat while increasing your muscle mass and strength.

A diet that is high in protein may also help lower blood pressure, fight diabetes, and more. The Reference Daily Intake (RDI) for protein is 46 grams for women and 56 grams for men. However, many health and fitness experts believe you need more than that to function optimally.

Eggs

- Whole eggs are among the healthiest and most nutritious foods available.
- They're an excellent source of vitamins, minerals, healthy fats, eye-protecting antioxidants, and brain nutrients that you need.
- Whole eggs are high in protein, but egg whites are almost pure protein.

- Egg and foods containing egg are not suitable for people with an egg allergy.
- Protein content: 33% of calories in a whole egg. One large egg has 6 grams of protein and 78 calories.

Almonds

- Almonds are a popular type of tree nut.
- They are rich in essential nutrients, including fiber, vitamin E, manganese, and magnesium.
- Almonds are not suitable for people who have a nut allergy.
- Protein content: 15% of calories. 6 grams and 164 calories per ounce.
- Other high protein nuts
- Pistachios (13% of calories) and cashews (11% of calories).

Chicken Breast

- Chicken breast is one of the most popular protein-rich foods.
- If you eat it without the skin, most of its calories come from protein.

- Chicken breast is also very easy to cook and versatile. It can taste delicious in a wide range of dishes.
- Protein content: 75% of calories. One roasted chicken breast without skin contains 53 grams and only 284 calories.

Oats

- Oats are among the healthiest grains available.
- They provide healthy fibers, magnesium, manganese, thiamine (vitamin B1), and several other nutrients.
- Protein content: 14% of calories. One cup of oats has 11 grams and 307 calories.

Cottage Cheese

- Cottage cheese is a type of cheese that is low in fat and calories.
- It's rich in calcium, phosphorus, selenium, vitamin B12, riboflavin (vitamin B2), and various other nutrients.
- Protein content: 69% of calories. One cup (226 grams) of low fat cottage cheese with 1% fat contains 28 grams of protein and 163 calories.

Other Types Of Cheese That Are High In Protein

Parmesan cheese (38% of calories), Swiss cheese (30%), mozzarella (29%), and cheddar (26%).

Greek Yogurt

Greek yogurt, also called strained yogurt, is a very thick type of yogurt.

It pairs well with sweet and savory dishes. It has a creamy texture and is high in many nutrients.

Protein content: 69% of calories. One 6-ounce (170-gram) container has 17 grams of protein and only 100 calories .

When buying Greek yogurt, opt for one without added sugar. Full fat Greek yogurt is also high in protein but contains more calories.

Similar options

Regular full fat yogurt (24% of calories) and kefir (40%).

Milk

Milk contains a little of nearly every nutrient that your body needs.

It's a good source of high quality protein, and it's high in calcium, phosphorus, and riboflavin (vitamin B2).

If you are concerned about your fat intake, low or zero fat milk is an option.

For those with lactose intolerance, consuming milk can lead to gastrointestinal symptoms. People with a milk allergy can likewise experience severe symptoms, so dairy milk is not a suitable option for them either.

For those who wish to drink milk but either cannot tolerate it or follow a purely plant-based diet, lternatives include soy milk.

Protein content: 21% of calories. One cup of whole milk contains 8 grams of protein and 149 calories. One cup of soy milk contains 6.3 grams of protein and 105 calories.

Broccoli

Broccoli is a healthy vegetable that provides vitamin C, vitamin K, fiber, and potassium.

It also provides bioactive nutrients that may help protect against cancer.

Calorie for calorie, it's high in protein compared with most vegetables.

Protein content: 33% of calories. One cup (96 grams) of chopped broccoli has 3 grams of protein and only 31 calories.

Lean Beef

Lean beef is high in protein, as well as highly bioavailable iron, vitamin B12, and large amounts of other vital nutrients.

Protein content: 53% of calories. One 3-ounce (85-gram) serving of lean sirloin steak contains 25 grams of protein and 186 calories.

Beef is suitable for people on a low carb diet.

Tuna

Tuna is a popular type of fish. You can eat it hot in a range of baked dishes or cold in salads.

It's low in fat and calories but a rich source of protein.

Like other fish, tuna is a good source of various nutrients and contains omega-3 fats.

Protein content: 84% of calories in tuna canned in water. One can (142 grams) contains 27 grams of protein and only 128 calories.

Quinoa

Quinoa is a popular pseudo-cereal that many consider a superfood.

It's rich in vitamins, minerals, fiber, and antioxidants.

Quinoa has numerous health benefits.

Protein content: 15% of calories. One cup (185 grams) of cooked quinoa has 8 grams and 222 calories.

Whey Protein Supplements

When you're pressed for time and unable to cook, a protein supplement can come in handy.

Whey protein is a high quality protein from dairy foods that can help build muscle mass. It may also aid weight loss.

If you'd like to try whey protein supplements, a large variety is available online.

Protein content: Varies between brands. Over 90% of the calories may be protein, and there may be 20-–50 grams of protein per serving.

Lentils

Lentils are a type of legume.

They are high in fiber, magnesium, potassium, iron, folate, copper, manganese, and various other nutrients.

Lentils are among the world's best sources of plant-based protein, and they're an excellent choice for vegetarians and vegans.

Protein content: 31% of calories. One cup (198 grams) of boiled lentils contains 18 grams and 230 calories.

Other High Protein Legumes

Soybeans (33% of calories), kidney beans (24%), and chickpeas (19%).

Ezekiel Bread

Ezekiel bread is different from most other breads.

It's made of organic and sprouted whole grains and legumes, including millet, barley, spelt, wheat, soybeans and lentils.

Compared with most breads, Ezekiel bread is high in protein, fiber, and various important nutrients.

Protein content: 20% of calories. One slice contains 4 grams and 80 calories.

Pumpkin Seeds

Pumpkins contain edible seeds called pumpkin seeds.

They're incredibly high in many nutrients, including iron, magnesium, and zinc.

Protein content: 22% of calories. One ounce (28 grams) has 9 grams of protein and 158 calories.

Flax seeds (12% of calories), sunflower seeds (12%), and chia seeds (11%).

Turkey Breast

Turkey breast is similar to chicken breast in many ways.

It consists mostly of protein, with very little fat and calories. It also tastes delicious and is high in various vitamins and minerals.

Protein content: 82% of calories. One 3-ounce (85-gram) serving contains 26 grams and 125 calories.

Fish (All Types)

Fish is healthy for various reasons.

It's rich in essential nutrients. Some types are high in heart-healthy omega-3 fatty acids.

Protein content: Highly variable. Salmon is 22% protein, containing 19 grams per 3-ounce (85- gram) serving and only 175 calories.

Shrimp

Shrimp is a type of seafood.

It's low in calories but high in various nutrients, including selenium and vitamin B12.

Like fish, shrimp contains omega-3 fatty acids.

Protein content: 97% of calories. A 3-ounce (85-gram) serving contains 20 grams and only 84 calories.

Brussels Sprouts

Brussels sprouts are another high protein vegetable related to broccoli.

They're high in fiber, vitamin C, and other nutrients.

Protein content: 28% of calories. One-half cup (78 grams) contains 2 grams of protein and 28 calories.

Peanuts

Peanuts are high in protein, fiber, and magnesium.

Studies show that they can help you lose weight.

Peanut butter is also high in protein, but it can likewise be high in calories. Therefore, you should eat it in moderation.

Peanuts are not suitable for people with a nut allergy.

Protein content: 18% of calories. One ounce (28 grams) contains 7 grams and 161 calories

High Protein Recipes

Miniature Omelettes With Ricotta

Ingredients

- 4 eggs
- Small handful flatleaf parsley, finely chopped, plus extra sprigs to serve
- Handful chives, finely snipped
- 1 small garlic clove, finely chopped
- 50g parmesan, freshly grated
- Olive oil, for frying
- For the filling
- 250g tub ricotta
- Handful fresh basil, torn
- 50g parmesan, freshly grated

Method

Beat the eggs with 2 tbsp water, then season if you want to. Mix in the parsley, chives, garlic and parmesan.

Heat a 23cm heavy-based frying pan on a medium heat with a little oil. When the oil's hot, add a ladleful (about a third) of the egg mixture and tip the mixture so it covers the base. Reduce the heat and cook the omelette until just firm, then flip it over and cook the other side. Keep warm. Repeat to make three omelettes, adding a little extra oil to the pan each time.

Make the filling by combining the ricotta, basil, parmesan and some pepper. Spread mixture over each omelette, roll up loosely like a cigar and cut into thickish slices. Can be made up to 5 hrs ahead. Serve garnished with parsley.

Herbed Chicken Skewers
Ingredients

- 500g tiny new potatoes - look for packets of tiny or baby new potatoes, or pick out the smallest ones you can find if they are sold loose
- 3 tbsp each of chopped parsley, mint and chives
- 6 tbsp olive oil
- 2 tbsp lemon juice
- 500g skinless chicken breasts, cut into 3cm chunks
- 1 red onion, peeled
- 1 red pepper, seeded and cut into 3cm chunks
- 1 lemon, cut into 8 wedges

For The Relish

- 8 ripe tomatoes - vine grown tomatoes tend to have the best flavour
- 2 green chillies, seeded and finely chopped
- 2 small garlic cloves, finely chopped
- 4 tbsp olive oil
- 2 tbsp white wine vinegar

Method

If using wooden or bamboo skewers soak eight in cold water for about half an hour. Cook the potatoes in boiling salted water for 10-12 minutes, until just tender, drain and leave to cool. Mix the herbs, oil, lemon juice, salt and pepper in a large bowl and add the chicken and potatoes. Mix well until everything is glistening. Cut the onion into 6 wedges, then separate the layers on each wedge. Add the onion and the pepper to the marinade and mix thoroughly.

To make the relish, halve and seed the tomatoes, then chop the flesh finely. Mix the tomatoes, chillies, garlic, oil, vinegar, salt and pepper and spoon into a small dish.

Thread the chicken, potatoes, peppers and onion onto 8 skewers, finishing each with a lemon wedge. Barbecue directly over a medium high heat for 5-6 minutes on each side, until the chicken is cooked. Serve piled on a serving platter with the tomato relish.

Dippy Eggs With Marmite Soldiers

Ingredients

- 2 eggs
- 4 slices wholemeal bread
- A knob of butter
- Marmite
- Mixed seeds

Method

Bring a pan of water to a simmer. Add 2 eggs, simmer for 2 mins if room temp, 3 mins if fridge-cold, then turn off heat. Cover the pan and leave for 2 mins more.

Meanwhile, toast 4 slices wholemeal bread and spread thinly with butter, then Marmite. To serve, cut into soldiers and dip into the egg, then a few mixed seeds.

Spiced Scrambled Eggs

Ingredients

- 1 small chopped onion

- 1 chopped red chilli
- Knob of butter
- 4 beaten eggs
- Splash of milk
- Good handful diced tomatoes
- Coriander leaves
- Toast, to serve

Method

Soften the onion and chilli in a knob of butter. Stir in the beaten eggs and a splash of milk. When nearly scrambled, gently stir in a good handful diced tomatoes followed by some coriander leaves. Season and eat on toast.

Thai Salmon Kebabs With Sweet Chilli & Lime Dip

Ingredients

- 4 tbsp sweet chilli sauce
- Juice 1 lime
- 4 x 140g/5oz skinless salmon fillet, cut into large chunks
- Oil, for drizzling

Method

Combine the sweet chilli sauce and lime juice in a bowl. Pour half the mixture into a bowl for serving. Thread the salmon onto 4 skewers and brush with the remaining chilli sauce. Marinate for 20 mins.

Heat a griddle pan until very hot. Shake excess marinade from the kebabs, then drizzle with oil, season and griddle for 8 mins, turning occasionally until the salmon is opaque and comes away easily from the pan. Serve hot with the dipping sauce.

One-Pan English Breakfast

Ingredients

- 4 good-quality pork chipolatas
- 4 rashers smoked back bacon
- 140g button mushroom
- 6 eggs, beaten
- 8 cherry tomatoes, halved
- Handful grated cheese (optional)
- 1 tbsp snipped chives

Method

Heat the grill to high. Heat a medium non-stick frying pan, add the chipolatas and fry for 3 mins. Add the bacon, turning occasionally, until it starts to crisp, about 5 mins more. Tip in the mushrooms and continue to cook for a further 3-5 mins. Drain any excess fat and move the ingredients so they are evenly spread out.

Season the eggs, then add to the pan, swirling to fill the spaces. Gently move with a fork for 2 mins over a low-medium heat until beginning to set. Scatter over the tomatoes, cheese, if using, and chives, then grill for 2 mins until set. Cut into wedges and serve with your favourite sauces.

Salmon & soya bean salad

Ingredients

- 1 large omega-3 rich egg (See TRY section at the bottom of the recipe)
- 200g frozen soya beans, defrosted
- Zest and juice 1 lemon
- 2 tbsp flax seed oil (we used granovita)
- 250g pouch Puy lentils
- Small bunch spring onions, sliced
- 2 poached salmon fillets, skin removed

Method

Put the egg in a pan, cover with cold water and bring to the boil. Cook for 4 mins (or 8 for hard-boiled), adding soya beans to the pan for the final min, then drain and run under cold water to cool. Shell and cut egg into 6 wedges, then set aside.

Mix the lemon juice and zest with the oil, season, then stir through the soya beans, lentils and spring onions.

Divide between 2 plates, then gently break the salmon into large flakes and put on top of the lentils along with the egg. Try it with seeded brown bread.

Vitality Chicken Salad With Avocado Dressing

Ingredients

- Handful frozen soya beans
- 1 skinless cooked chicken breast, shredded
- ¼ cucumber, peeled, deseeded and chopped
- ½ avocado, flesh scooped out
- Few drops tabasco sauce
- Juice ½ lemon, plus a lemon wedge
- 2 tsp extra-virgin olive oil
- 5-6 little gem lettuce leaves
- 1 tsp mixed seed

Method

Blanch the soya beans for 3 mins. Rinse in cold water and drain thoroughly. Put the chicken, beans and cucumber in a bowl.

Blitz the avocado, Tabasco, lemon juice and oil in a food processor or with a hand blender. Season, pour into the bowl and mix well to coat.

Spoon the mixture into the lettuce leaves (or serve it alongside them) and sprinkle with the seeds. Chill until lunch, then serve with a lemon wedge.

Griddled Chicken With quinoa Greek Salad

Ingredients

- 225g quinoa
- 25g butter
- 1 red chilli, deseeded and finely chopped
- 1 garlic clove, crushed
- 400g chicken
- Mini fillets
- 1½ tbsp extra-virgin olive oil

- 300g vine tomato, roughly chopped
- Handful pitted black kalamata olive
- 1 red onion, finely sliced
- 100g feta cheese, crumbled
- Small bunch mint
- Leaves, chopped
- Juice and zest ½ lemon

Method

Cook the quinoa following the pack instructions, then rinse in cold water and drain thoroughly.

Meanwhile, mix the butter, chilli and garlic into a paste. Toss the chicken fillets in 2 tsp of the olive oil with some seasoning. Lay in a hot griddle pan and cook for 3-4 mins each side or until cooked through. Transfer to a plate, dot with the spicy butter and set aside to melt.

Next, tip the tomatoes, olives, onion, feta and mint into a bowl. Toss in the cooked quinoa. Stir through the remaining olive oil, lemon juice and zest, and season well. Serve with the chicken fillets on top, drizzled with any buttery chicken juices.

Cajun Turkey Steaks With Pineapple Salsa

Ingredients

- 1 red onion, finely chopped
- 1 tbsp sunflower oil
- 1 red pepper, deseeded and diced
- 200g basmati rice
- 450ml chicken stock
- 400g can kidney bean, rinsed and drained
- 4 turkey
- Steaks
- 2 tsp cajun seasoning
- 5oz 140g fresh pineapple
- (or 220g can pineapple rings, drained)
- ½ green chilli, finely chopped
- Juice 1 lime

Method

Reserve 2 tbsp of the onion for the salsa. Heat the oil in a saucepan and cook the remaining onion and half the pepper for 4 mins or until softened and coloured. Stir in the rice, then pour in the stock. Add the kidney beans and a pinch of salt. Bring to the boil, stir once, cover the pan, and then reduce the heat to a gentle simmer. Cook for 15 mins until the rice is tender and the liquid absorbed.

Dust the turkey steaks with the Cajun spice and griddle or fry in a non-stick pan for about 4-6 mins on each side until cooked through. Cut the pineapple into small pieces and mix together with the reserved red onion, pepper, green chilli and lime juice. Spoon some salsa over each steak and serve with the rice.

Spicy Cajun Chicken quinoa

Ingredients

- 4 skinless chicken breasts, cut into bite-sized pieces
- 1 tbsp cajun seasoning
- 100g quinoa
- 600ml hot chicken stock
- 100g dried apricots, sliced
- ½ x 250g pouch ready-to-use puy lentils
- 1 tbsp olive oil
- 2 red onions, cut into thin wedges
- 1 bunch spring onions, chopped
- Small bunch coriander, chopped

Method

Heat oven to 200C/180C fan/gas 6. Toss the chicken with the Cajun spice and arrange in a single layer in a roasting tin.Bake for 20 mins until the chicken is cooked.Set aside.Meanwhile, cook the quinoa in the chicken stock for 15 mins until tender, adding the apricots and lentils for the final 5 mins. Drain and place into a large bowl with the chicken, toss together.

While the quinoa is cooking, heat the oil in a large frying pan and soften the onions for 10-15 mins. Toss the onions into the quinoa with the coriander and some seasoning, then mix well.

Spring Salmon With Minty Veg

Ingredients

- 750g small new potato, thickly sliced
- 750g frozen pea and beans (we used waitrose pea and bean mix, £2.29/1kg)
- 3 tbsp olive oil
- Zest and juice of 1 lemon
- Small pack mint, leaves only
- 4 salmon fillets about 140g/5oz each

Method

Boil the potatoes in a large pan for 4 mins. Tip in the peas and beans, bring back up to a boil, then carry on cooking for another 3 mins until the potatoes and beans are tender. Whizz the olive oil, lemon zest and juice and mint in a blender to make a dressing(or finely chop the mint and whisk into the oil and lemon).

Put the salmon in a microwave-proof dish, season, then pour the dressing over.Cover with cling film, pierce, then microwave on High for 4-5 mins until cooked through. Drain the veg, then mix with the hot dressing and cooking juices from the fish. Serve the fish on top of the vegetables.

Simple Seafood Chowder
Ingredients

- 1 tbsp vegetable oil
- 1 large onion, chopped
- 100g streaky bacon, chopped
- 1 tbsp plain flour
- 600ml fish stock, made from 1 fish stock cube
- 225g new potato, halved
- Pinch mace
- Pinch cayenne pepper

- 300ml milk
- 320g pack fish pie mix (salmon, haddock and smoked haddock)
- 4 tbsp single cream
- 250g pack cooked mixed shellfish
- Small bunch parsley, chopped
- Crusty bread, to serve

Method

Heat the oil in a large saucepan over a medium heat, then add the onion and bacon. Cook for 8-10 mins until the onion is soft and the bacon is cooked. Stir in the flour, then cook for a further 2 mins.

Pour in the fish stock and bring it up to a gentle simmer. Add the potatoes, cover, then simmer for 10-12 mins until the potatoes are cooked through.

Add the mace, cayenne pepper and some seasoning, then stir in the milk.

Tip the fish pie mix into the pan, gently simmer for 4 mins. Add the cream and shellfish, then simmer for 1 min more. Check the seasoning. Sprinkle with the parsley and serve with some crusty bread.

Sea Bass & Seafood Italian One-Pot

Ingredients

- 2 tbsp olive oil
- 1 fennel bulb, halved and sliced, fronds kept separate to garnish
- 2 garlic cloves, sliced
- ½ red chilli, chopped
- 250g cleaned squid, sliced into rings
- Bunch basil, leaves and stalks separated, stalks tied together, leaves roughly chopped
- 400g can chopped tomato
- 150ml white wine
- 2 large handfuls of mussels or clams
- 8 large raw prawns
- (whole look nicest)
- 4 sea bass fillets (about 140g/5oz each)
- Crusty bread, to serve

Method

Heat the oil in a large saucepan with a tight-fitting lid, then add the fennel, garlic and chilli. Fry until softened, then add the squid, basil stalks, tomatoes and wine. Simmer over a low heat for 35 mins until the squid is tender and the sauce has thickened slightly, then season.

Scatter the mussels and prawns over the sauce, lay the sea bass fillets on top, cover, turn up the heat and cook hard for 5 mins. Serve scattered with the basil leaves and fennel fronds, with crusty bread.

Fruity LAMB TAGINE
Ingredients

- 2 tbsp olive oil
- 500g lean diced lamb
- 1 large onion, roughly chopped
- 2 large carrots, quartered lengthways and cut into chunks
- 2 garlic cloves, finely chopped
- 2 tbsp ras-el-hanout spice mix
- 400g can chopped tomato
- 400g can chickpea, rinsed and drained
- 200g dried apricot

- 600ml chicken stock
- To serve
- 120g pack pomegranate
- Seeds
- 2 large handfuls coriander, roughly chopped

Method

Heat oven to 180C/160C fan/gas 4.Heat the oil in a casserole and brown the lamb on all sides.Scoop the lamb out onto a plate, then add the onion and carrots and cook for 2-3 mins until golden.

Add the garlic and cook for 1 min more. Stir in the spices and tomatoes, and season.Tip the lamb back in with the chickpeas and apricots. Pour over the stock, stir and bring to a simmer. Cover the dish and place in the oven for 1 hr.

If the lamb is still a little tough, give it 20 mins more until tender. When ready, leave it to rest so it's not piping hot, then serve scattered with pomegranate and herbs, with couscous or rice alongside.

Chicken, Red Pepper & Almond Traybake
Ingredients

- 500g boneless, skinless chicken thigh
- 3 medium red onions, cut into thick wedges
- 500g small red potato, cut into thick slices
- 2 red peppers, deseeded and cut into thick slices
- 1 garlic clove, finely chopped
- 1 tsp each ground cumin, smoked paprika and fennel seeds, slightly crushed
- 3 tbsp olive oil
- Zest and juice 1 lemon
- 50g whole blanched almond, roughly chopped
- 170g tub 0% greek yogurt, to serve
- Small handful parsley
- Or coriander, chopped, to serve

Method

Heat oven to 200C/180C fan/gas 6. Place the chicken, onions, potatoes and peppers in a large bowl and season. in another bowl, mix together the garlic, spices, oil, and lemon zest and juice. Pour this over everything and spread the mixture between 2 baking trays.

Roast for 40 mins, turning over after 20 mins, until the chicken is cooked through. Add the almonds for the final 8 mins of cooking. Serve in bowls with a big dollop of Greek yogurt and some chopped parsley or coriander.

Mexican Bean Chilli

Ingredients

- 1 onion, diced
- 1 red pepper, diced
- 1 tbsp olive oil
- 1 tsp chilli powder
- 500g beef mince
- 415g can baked beans
- 150ml beef stock
- 1 tbsp chipotle paste
- Coriander leaves, rice and yogurt, to serve

Method

Fry the onion and red pepper in olive oil over a medium heat for 10-15 mins or until softened. Increase the heat, add the chilli powder and cook for a few minutes before adding the mince. Cook until browned and all the liquid has evaporated.

Tip in the baked beans, beef stock and chipotle paste.Simmer over a low heat for 15-20 mins. Season, scatter with coriander leaves and serve with rice and yogurt.

Conclusion

There are many potential sources of protein people can choose from when trying to lose weight. Many protein sources offer additional nutrients that benefit overall health as well.

Printed in Great Britain
by Amazon